ELK

Published by Smart Apple Media
1980 Lookout Drive, North Mankato, Minnesota 56003

Design and Production by The Design Lab/Kathy Petelinsek

Photographs by D. Robert Franz, Michael Mauro, Tom Stack & Associates, Visuals Unlimited

Library of Congress Cataloging-in-Publication Data
Wrobel, Scott.
Elk / by Scott Wrobel
p. cm. — (Northern Trek)
Includes resources, glossary, and index
Summary: Discusses the history of the North American elk, its physical
characteristics and habits, and efforts to preserve the species.
ISBN 1-58340-033-8
1. Elk—Juvenile literature. [1. Elk.] I. Title. II. Series: Northern Trek (Mankato, Minn.)

QL737.U55W76   2000
599.65'7—dc21   99-29935
First Edition

2 4 6 8 9 7 5 3 1

NORTHERN TREK

ELK

WRITTEN BY SCOTT WROBEL

SMART APPLE MEDIA

In the mountains and deep forests of the north, the cool winds of fall carry the echoing bugle of the mighty elk. Like a loon's cry or a wolf's howl, an elk's bugle is one of nature's most unforgettable songs. For thousands of years, it was heard by people living all across most of North America. Strong and beautiful, elk have long been a symbol of the northern wilderness. Today, even though the elk population is much smaller than it once was, many of these majestic animals continue to fill the northern woods with their haunting calls.

KERRISDALE BRANCH

THE ELK (*Cervus canadensis*) belongs to the same family of mammals as caribou, white-tailed deer, mule deer, and moose. Male elk, called bulls, can weigh up to 770 pounds (350 kg) and stand about five feet (1.5 m) tall at the shoulder. Females, or cows, are slightly shorter and may weigh 500 pounds (225 kg). Elk have long, powerful legs. Running speed helps the elk to escape **predators** such as wolves and mountain lions, and **endurance** allows them to **migrate** long distances to find food.

The elk's coat ranges in color from deep brown to light tan, and its legs and neck are often darker than its body. The Shawnee Indians called the elk *wapiti*, which means "white rump," because its hind end is a light beige color. In the spring, elk shed their winter coats and grow short summer coats. In September, their warm coats grow back just in time for winter.

Elk have impressive antlers. In the spring,

When it sheds its winter coat, the elk's thick fur peels away in chunks and is completely gone by July.

antlers grow from bony lumps on the skulls of bulls. In the early stages of growth, the antlers are made of **cartilage** and are protected by a soft covering of skin. Throughout spring and summer, the antlers grow up to one inch (2.5 cm) a day. By August, they harden into bone. In the fall, after the **rutting season**, the bulls shed their antlers.

Bulls grow new and bigger sets of antlers with each passing year. Spiked points, called tines, grow in the same way that branches grow from tree trunks. By a bull's sixth or seventh year, his antlers may have six tines that are each 10 to 20 inches (25-50 cm) long. Full-grown antlers may measure five feet (1.5 m) across and weigh up to 40 pounds (18 kg).

The skin covering antlers, called velvet, helps the antlers grow. The velvet then dries up and the elk rubs it off against trees or on the ground.

Elk antlers, which turn white lying in the sun, are valuable to many people. Artists may carve them into jewelry or make furniture out of them. Some people even grind them up to make natural medicines.

Elk have keen senses that enable them to detect predators. They can spot the slightest movement, and their ears twitch back and forth to pick up even the faintest noise. Elk also have a strong sense of smell.

Elk gather wherever there is shelter, food, and water. Grouped under tall trees, elk stay warm together in the winter and are shaded from the sun in the summer. Elk also need shelter to hide from predators. Steep canyons, valleys, and rock heaps

---

Elk spend most of their time grazing, but they also need to be near lakes or rivers to drink and to cool their bodies off.

Large bull elks don't always fight during mating season. They may march side by side, then suddenly turn away. If they do fight, they lock antlers and try to drive each other backward until one of them gives up.

are good places for herds to gather. A full-grown elk needs to eat up to 15 pounds (6.8 kg) of food per day. In the winter, elk eat plants, twigs, roots, bark, and pine needles. In the warmer months, they rely on grass and soft-stemmed plants.

Elk bulls and cows live in separate herds for most of the year. They come together only to mate in late summer and early fall. By the middle of the **rutting season**, a bull's antlers are fully grown and ready for fighting. This is also when bulls begin their bugling. Cows will mate with only the strongest, most healthiest males, and they listen to bugles for hints about the bull. Each male's bugle sounds a little different; the older and larger the bull, the louder the sound.

Bulls listen for the bugles of other males as well. They bellow back to challenge them. They also try to frighten other males with a display of head-shaking and ground-scuffing. Young males—those under six years old—usually retreat when challenged. Bulls of equal size and age may thrash the ground with their antlers before locking together in battle. Such fights are simply tests of strength—the elk usually are not harmed.

Once elks have mated, it takes about eight and a half months for a baby elk to develop inside its mother. Calves are born between May and early July. A newborn calf can weigh 35 pounds (16 kg).

Elk bugling may attract predators, so to protect herself and her young, a female elk may leave the herd.

It will gain about two pounds (1 kg) per day during the first few weeks of its life. Young calves have **camouflaged** coats and no noticeable odor, which helps them to hide from enemies. Still, cows often lose their calves to bears, coyotes, or wolves. If a calf survives its first few weeks, it can then run fast enough to escape most predators.

Long before European settlers moved to North America, elk numbered more than 100 million. The first humans to coexist with elk were Native Americans, who depended on them for many things. Elk meat was eaten, antlers and bones were carved into weapons, and hides were used to make clothing and homes. Northwest

Young elk grow fast. At the start of its first winter, a calf can weigh five times as much as it did at birth. It will have lost its spots and grown a thick coat of fur.

Elk are strong runners and can cover great distances to outrun predators. But herd life is not based on fear of danger. Lively and playful, both adult and young elk may leap, kick, and chase each other for fun.

coastal tribes used elk bones and antlers to make fishing spears.

In the late 1800s, many ranchers and farmers settled in the western United States. Elk often ate crops or livestock food, so the settlers began to kill the elk. Soon, the elk population dropped. People began to fear that too many elk were being killed. In the early 1900s, people began trying to increase the number of elk. This was done by **reintroducing** several herds into Yellowstone National Park.

Since 1920, the elk population has continued to rise with the help of conservation groups and other concerned people. Today, most elk live in the western parts of Canada and the United States, many along the Rocky Mountains. Some elk live as far east as Pennsylvania.

Elk are also being raised by people on ranch-es. More than 20,000 elk live behind fences on ranches where they are raised for their meat and antlers. Since elk continue to live with growing numbers of humans, their future is dependent on people working to help them. As long as people continue looking out for them, elk and other wildlife will remain a valuable part of the natural world.

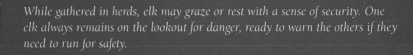
While gathered in herds, elk may graze or rest with a sense of security. One elk always remains on the lookout for danger, ready to warn the others if they need to run for safety.

ELK HERDS ROAM OVER

vast areas of land, so finding them is usually not easy; however, once you locate them, you will often see many together. The best viewing areas are national and state parks in the western and central United States.

With the help of people and the government, the elk population is continuing to grow. Listed here are various elk habitats with public access. As with any trek into nature, it is important to remember that wild animals are unpredictable and can be dangerous if approached. The best way to view wildlife is from a respectful—and safe—distance.

NATIONAL ELK RANGE IN JACKSON, WYOMING

The most popular and most populous elk herds (more than 17,000) in North America are located here, at the edge of Grand Teton National Park and just south of Yellowstone National Park. In the summer, the herds are in the higher summer range of the Jackson Hole Valley up into the Tetons and South Yellowstone.

BANFF NATIONAL PARK IN ALBERTA, CANADA

Thousands of elk roam this beautiful national park. The Vermilion Lakes Drive and the Buffalo Paddock are both excellent areas to watch elk.

SIZERVILLE STATE PARK IN EMPORIUM, PENNSYLVANIA

Located seven miles north of Emporium, the park is surrounded by the Susquehannock State Forest—nearly a half-million acres (202,000 h) where elk roam.

CHEQUAMEGON NATIONAL FOREST, CLAM LAKE, WISCONSIN

Elk have been reintroduced to this 719 square miles (1,862 km²) of forest, an area where they once roamed freely before human habitation.

camouflaged: *something that imitates the appearance of its surroundings*

cartilage: *an elastic tissue often found at the joints between bones*

endurance: *the ability to run a long distance before getting tired*

migrate: *to move from one place to another, usually to feed*

predators: *animals that kill other animals for food*

reintroducing: *moving animals back into an area where they once lived*

rutting season: *a time of the year when male animals become aggressive and prepare to mate*